✪ WEAPONS OF WAR
ATTACK
AND TRANSPORT
AIRCRAFT
1945 TO TODAY

A⁺
Smart Apple Media

Published by arrangement with Amber Books

Contributing authors: Chris Chant, Steve Crawford, Martin J. Dougherty,
Ian Hogg, Robert Jackson, Chris McNab, Michael Sharpe, Philip Trewhitt

Special thanks to series consultant Dr. Steve Potts

Photo credits: Art-Tech/Aerospace, Cody Images, Corbis, U.S. Department of Defense,
except page 15, courtesy of Personal Collection/Newton Hucke.

Illustrations: © Art-Tech/Aerospace

Library of Congress Cataloging-in-Publication Data

Sharpe, Mike, 1970-
Attack & transport aircraft : 1945 to today / Michael Sharpe.
pages cm. — (Weapons of war)
Includes index.
ISBN 978-1-62588-042-0
1. Attack planes — History. 2. Transport planes — History. I. Title.
UG1242.A28S49 2015
623.74'63 – dc23
                              2013032031

Printed in the United States at Corporate Graphics,
North Mankato, Minnesota
PO1649
2-2014

9 8 7 6 5 4 3 2 1

CONTENTS

Introduction

Strike Force

Attack aircraft give armed services a form of "flying artillery", while transport aircraft improves mobility and logistics.

The attack, or strike, aircraft occupies a very specific position in the history of millitary aircraft. To many, the strike aircraft can often appear little different from a regular fighter aircraft. Indeed, on many occasions the attack aircraft can simply be a version of another type. For example, the fearsome F-4A Phantom has been produced in air-superiority and specialist ground-attack versions, but both are based around the same essential airframe. For many years (especially during the World Wars era) there was little to distinguish between a fighter or light bomber and a dedicated strike aircraft. Sometimes the difference between aircraft would be little more than a couple of underwing hardpoints for light bombs.

Yet since the introduction of strike aircraft during World War I, lessons have been learned about the nature of the attack aircraft. A partial list of the criteria for effective attack aircraft would include: improved armor around the pilot to protect from ground fire; radar and navigation systems configured for low-level approaches and attack runs; excellent systems for communicating with ground forces; weapon systems designed specifically for ground

A-4 SKYHAWK: see page 45

WEAPONS OF WAR

F-105 THUNDERCHIEF: see page 53

targets, such as armored vehicles and reinforced emplacements; designation and targeting systems suitable for such targets; fuel capacity to reach distant land targets; and, of course, air crew trained in the art of ground-attack missions.

Properly configured, the strike/attack aircraft is undoubtedly a menacing presence above the battlefield, and it has been essential to the outcome of many major battles and campaigns. From the skies over Normandy in 1944 to those over Afghanistan in 2014, the attack aircraft has made the operations of enemy ground forces a frequently harrowing experience.

ATTACK CONCEPT

When World War II finally came to a close in September 1945, there was no doubt that the prop-powered attack aircraft had truly proved its worth. The global conflict had demonstrated that heavily armed attack aircraft, properly coordinated with ground forces, could inflict devastating attacks and operational delays upon an enemy. Noticable troop movements along routes open to attack-aircraft predation could prove almost suicidal in some theatres, such as in Normandy in the summer of 1944. Aircraft such as the Hawker Typhoon, Republic P-47 Thunderbolt, Douglas A-20 Havoc, Junkers Ju 87 Stuka, and Ilyushin Il-2 carried a heavy mix of machine guns, cannon, rockets, and bombs, plus had the armor and speed to give at least a decent chance of surviving. Yet as the 1940s gave way to the 1950s, the concept of the attack aircraft would go through a period of uncertainty as it attempted to find its place in the age of the jet and nuclear weapons.

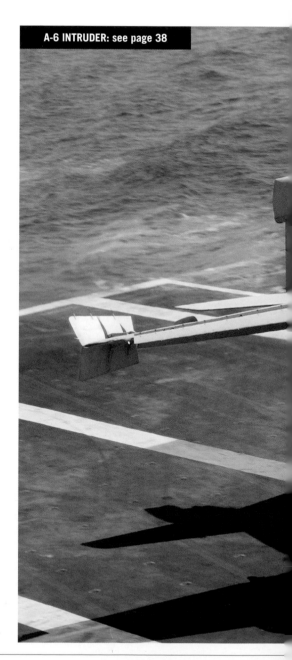

A-6 INTRUDER: see page 38

VULCAN: see page 25

Although first introduced into combat in 1944, jet fighters only came into their own during the Korean War (1950–53).

LOW-LEVEL POWER

The 1950s and 1960s were a curious time in the history of attack aircraft design. As the Cold War intensified, and the focus of air forces shifted to delivering, or stopping, nuclear-tipped air attacks, the tactical support aircraft became somewhat sidelined by long-range nuclear bombers and high-speed, high-altitude jet interceptors. Nevertheless, conflicts such as those in Korea (1950—53) and Vietnam (1954—75) quickly proved that the ground-attack aircraft still had a vital role

to play in delivering close support.

From the US perspective, the range of attack aircraft that emerged during the 1950s and 1960s provides a fascinating insight into aircraft development policy. Even in an age of high-performance jets, one of the most prolific US attack aircraft was the Douglas A-1 Skyraider. The Skyraider was a piston-engined aircraft with a top speed of just 322 mph (518 km/h), yet it would serve with distinction in combat throughout the Vietnam War. Its skills as a ground-attack aircraft were exceptional

B-52 STRATOFORTRESS: see page 27

resilience (aircraft with huge holes in their wings and fuselages routinely made it back to base), powerful weapons (4 x 20mm cannon and up to 8,000 lb. [3,600 kg] of external ordnance) and, ironically, its slow speed. Faster jet-powered attack aircraft such as the Republic F-105 Thunderchief — which could carry a 14,000 lb. (6,400 kg) bombload at speeds of up to Mach 2 — often struggled to identify and attack targets in the convoluted Vietnamese landscape when flying at speeds approaching or exceeding the speed of sound. The Skyraider, by contrast, could maneuver with exceptional mobility at tree-top height and drop its bombs down into the smallest clearings.

The Skyraider demonstrated that the era of the prop-powered attack aircraft was not yet over, but the Vietnam War did see the transition to jets take place in earnest. The McDonnell-Douglas A-4 Skyhawk, Grumman A-6 Intruder and Vought A-7 Corsair II became the principal attack aircraft of the US armed services during the conflict. All were subsonic jets with heavy ordnance loads, although the hot and humid conditions of Vietnam often robbed them of some of the performance they enjoyed in colder environments back home. Yet this breed of attack aircraft also now sat alongside a fresh generation of multi-role aircraft. The best representative of this type during the 1960s

WEAPONS OF WAR

SUPER ETENDARD: see page 30

was the McDonnell Douglas F-4 Phantom. Developed by McDonnell during the 1950s, the F-4 was initially was an air superiority fighter in the US Navy. However, its capability as a robust and fast fighter-bomber was quickly recognized, and multi-role versions began serving not only with the US Navy and US Air Force, but also with export customers such as the United Kingdom, Germany, Japan, Israel, and Spain.

The Phantom has such an honored place in the history of Cold War aviation because it could switch from engaging enemy aircraft at speeds exceeding Mach 2 to making low-level and low-speed napalm runs on isolated jungle targets. Like the attack aircraft listed above, the F-4 in attack mode also featured a new generation of precision-guided munitions (PGMs) that were developed in the 1960s and 70s. Bombs such as the laser-guided Paveway and television-guided Walleye transformed the accuracy with which attack aircraft could strike point targets such as bunkers or bridges. More versions of the aircraft were produced in the 1970s, notably the F-4G "Wild Weasel", which was designed principally to suppress surface-to-air missile (SAM) and anti-aircraft radar facilities.

By the end of the US involvement in Vietnam in 1975, the United States had an impressive aerial arsenal of attack aircraft. The days of the Skyraider had ended, and the advanced jet strike aircraft was established. But the United States was not the only country to develop its attack capability.

INTERNATIONAL DEVELOPMENTS

Ever watchful of events among the Western forces, the Soviet Union ensured that it also fielded a range of jet-powered attack aircraft

JAGUAR: see page 54

AMX: see page 24

The attack aircraft not only had to deliver heavy, accurate air-to-ground fire, it also had to demonstrate survivability.

during the 1950s and 1960s. One of the first was the Sukhoi Su-7, which was designed as a supersonic fighter in 1955. The aircraft struggled to meet fighter requirements, however, so it was reconfigured for a low-altitude attack role, which manifested itself in the Su-7B in 1958. The Su-7B became the dominant Soviet attack aircraft of the 1960s, and was widely exported, particularly to the Middle East and India, where it demonstrated an unimpressive combat performance. (One notable problem was that the poor cockpit design led to pilots positioning themselves awkwardly in the seat, resulting in fatal injuries if they had to eject suddenly.) The Su-7B was largely replaced by the Sukhoi Su-1/

in the 1970s, this aircraft offering improved take-off and landing performance and better firepower. Like its predecessor — and indeed many of the Soviet-era jets — the Su-17 enjoyed widespread export success. The United Kingdom also invested in new attack aircraft, yet in the context of a confused and inefficient policy towards developing its Cold War air fleet. In terms of purely home-grown attack aircraft, the typical UK post-war attack aircraft was the Blackburn/Hawker Siddeley Buccaneer. The Buccaneer received poor reviews during its service life. It was an ungainly aircraft to look at, and its maximum speed was 690 mph (1,110 km/h) — such speeds didn't exactly catch the imagination in

SU-20: see page 55

an era of supersonic flight. Yet the Buccaneer had much to its credit as an attack aircraft. Its slow speed and sturdy design gave it the excellent low-level maneuverability which helped it elude enemy attack. It could handle more than 12,000 pounds (5,400 kg) of ordnance — in fact, the Buccaneer could actually fly faster than a Mirage or Phantom when the aircraft were carrying the same loads. The Buccaneer had such a reliable design that it served on in various capacities until the mid 1990s.

The UK's other major strike aircraft during the 1970s was the far more streamlined SEPECAT Jaguar, although this was a joint Anglo-French venture. Unlike the Buccaneer, the Jaguar was a supersonic aircraft, and was capable of delivering nuclear strikes. It was strictly a multi-role aircraft, and it became one of the UK's most versatile aircraft of the 1970s. It shared that distinction with the vertical/short takeoff and landing (V/STOL) Hawker Siddeley Harrier, an aircraft that offered exceptional flexibility of roles whether operating from land or from an aircraft carrier. The Harrier also became a significant component of the US Navy during the 1970s, providing an additional carrier-borne strike aircraft, and it proved its worth in combat during the Falklands War of 1982, although principally in a naval air defense role rather than as an attack aircraft.

STATE OF THE ART

The period from 1970 to the present has been startling in terms of all areas of aircraft development, not just attack types. In many ways, the dedicated attack aircraft has become somewhat rarer; it is now more common for the attack role to be included

TU-22M: see page 57

A-10 THUNDERBOLT II: see page 36

WEAPONS OF WAR

B-2 SPIRIT: see page 51

In the 1970s, attack aircraft became precision weapon delivery systems, capable of striking pinpoint targets.

in all-weather multi-role platforms. Good examples of such aircraft to emerge during this era include the Panavia Tornado, the General Dynamics Γ 111, the Dassault-Breguet mirage F.1, the Saab AJ37 Viggen (actually an attack aircraft with a secondary interceptor role) and the McDonnell Douglas F-15 Eagle. These supersonic powerhouses, however, have not entirely excluded the production of more specifically attack-focused aircraft. The Fairchild A-10 Thunderbolt, for example, stands as a monstrous counterpoint. Subsonic by design — its maximum speed is just 439 mph (706 km/h) — the A-10 mounts a tank-destroying 30mm cannon and 16,000 pounds (7,258 kg) of ordnance. Its primary purpose is as an anti-armor vehicle, a role it fulfilled to perfection in the Middle East conflicts of 1990–91 and 2003–11. The A-10 is soon to be replaced in service, but it will be hard to replace.

The attack aircraft of the future will likely be stealth varieties, building on the characteristics of stealth bombers such as the F-117 Nighthawk. Sophisticated aircraft like the F-22 Raptor and Eurofighter Typhoon have taken over much attack responsibility, but few would argue that unmanned aerial vehicles (UAVs, commonly known as drones) are the future for the attack aircraft. In fact, UAVs, first used by the US in armed attacks in 2001, have already been established as

CF-17 GLOBEMASTER: see page 46

WEAPONS OF WAR

C-5A GALAXY: see page 43

an integral part of US military operations. The Predator and the Reaper, both carrying powerful missiles, have been successful in combat missions in Afghanistan. By 2012, the US Air Force trained more UAV pilots than ordinary jet fighter pilots. They ultimately offer the best of all worlds — a high-performance attack platform, without the risk of putting a pilot in harm's way.

TRANSPORT AIRCRAFT

This book also studies transport aircraft. Although less exciting than attack aircraft, the transport aircraft performs no less a vital role. Indeed, the sheer importance of logistics in sustaining operations means that the transport aircraft has a valid argument to being military aviation's most important type of equipment. Today's forces can find themselves deployed an ocean away at a moment's notice. Transport aircraft not only allow them to do so in large numbers and within a few hours, but the carrying capacity of some of the larger types means heavy equipment — even up to main battle tanks — can go with them. For example, the Boeing C-17 Globemaster aircraft can carry 170,900 lb. (77,517 kg) of cargo in configurations that can include 134 troops, an M1 Abrams tank or three Styker armored vehicles, and it has a range of 2,785 miles (4,482 km). Several of these aircraft, therefore, could deploy a battalion of troops and a unit of armored vehicles.

Of course, not all transport aircraft are of such impressive dimensions. Much aerial logistics work is performed by helicopters and turboprop-powered workhorses such as the C-130 Hercules. What they all ensure, however, is that armies can operate remotely from home nations or main bases. Like attack aircraft, transport aircraft have dramatically changed warfare.

SUPER TUCANO: see page 34

R-99 (ERJ 145): see page 32

AMX International AMX

The AMX International AMX is the product of a collaboration between the Italian companies of Aeritalia and Aermacchi and the Brazilian EMBRAER company. It was born out of a requirement that the indigenous air forces of both countries had in the early 1980s for a small tactical fighter bomber, to replace Fiat G91s, F104Gs, and EMBRAER AT-26 Xavantes respectively. A Piaggio built Rolls-Royce tubofan was chosen as the powerplant for the compact and attractive little fighter. The first prototype flew in May 1984 and, by 1990, the seven development aircraft had accumulated more than 2500 hours. Aeritalia are responsible for approximately 50 percent of the work, including the major assemblies, with the other two partners completing all other sections. The aircraft entered service with the Aeronautica Italia Militare in April 1989.

SPECIFICATIONS

COUNTRY OF ORIGIN: Italy and Brazil
TYPE: single-seat multi-role combat aircraft
POWERPLANT: 11,030 pounds (1 x 5003 kg) Fiat/Piaggio/Alfa Romeo (Rolls Royce) Spey Mk 807 turbofan
PERFORMANCE: maximum speed 651 mph (1047 km/h); service ceiling 42,650 feet (13,000 m); combat radius at low level 345 miles (556 km)
WEIGHTS: empty 14,771 pounds (6700 kg); maximum take-off 28,660 pounds (13,000 kg)
WINGSPAN: 29 feet 1 inch (8.87 m)
LENGTH: 43 feet 5 inches (13.23 m)
HEIGHT: 14 feet 11 inches (4.55 m);
WING AREA: 226.04 feet^2 (21 m^2)
ARMAMENT: 1 x 20 mm General Dynamics M61A1 cannon or 2 x 30 mm DEFA cannon (on Brazilian version); 5 x exernal hardpoints with provision for up to 8377 pounds (3800 kg) of stores; 2 x wing tip rails for Sidewinder or similar air-to-air missiles

Avro Vulcan B.Mk 2

In the early 1950s, the British Royal Air Force issued Specification B.14/46, which called for an aircraft that could deliver nuclear weapons from any of its bases in the world. The Avro Vulcan was thus designed ostensibly as a high level nuclear bomber. The first production aircraft were designated B.Mk 1 and entered service in this role in 1956 with the V-bomber force. The B.Mk 1 was joined in service in 1960 by the improved Vulcan B.Mk 2. These aircraft were furnished with inflight refueling equipment. It was also intended that this version would carry the Blue Steel or American Skybolt stand-off nuclear weapons, but, with the adoption of Polaris, these plans never materialized. Existing Vulcan squadrons converted to the B.Mk 2A in 1962-64 This aircraft wears the bat emblem of No. 9 Squadron and was later converted to B.Mk 2A standard.

SPECIFICATIONS

COUNTRY OF ORIGIN: United Kingdom
TYPE: long-range strategic bomber
POWERPLANT: 4 x 17,000 pounds (7711 kg) Rolls-Royce Olympus 201
PERFORMANCE: maximum speed at altitude 645 mph (1038 km/h); service ceiling 65,000 feet (19,810 m); range with normal bomb load 4600 miles (7403 km)
WEIGHTS: maximum take-off weight 250,000 pounds (113,398 kg)
WINGSPAN: 111 feet (33.83 m)
LENGTH: 99 feet 11 inches (30.45 m)
HEIGHT: 27 feet 2 inches (8.28 m)
WING AREA: 3964 feet^2 (368.26m^2)
ARMAMENT: internal bay with provision for up to 47,198 pounds (21,454 kg) of bombs

BAe/MD Harrier GR.Mk 7

The collaboration of BAe and McDonnell Douglas resulted from a desire to improve the limited range/payload capability of the AV-8A operated by the US Marine Corps and Harrier GR.Mk 3. The resulting aircraft were tailored specifically to the needs of each service. The GR.Mk 5 differs in several ways from its predecessor. A wider wing made of composite materials permits the carriage of an extra 2000 pounds (907 kg) of fuel, while revised wing control surfaces generate greater lift. In the cockpit, the GR.Mk 5 has a more complex avionics fit, with moving map display and IR sensor. Two extra wing pylons are fitted for Sidewinder missiles. The GR.Mk 5 made its service debut in November 1988 and was followed by the GR.Mk 7.

SPECIFICATIONS

COUNTRY OF ORIGIN: UK and US
TYPE: V/STOL close-support aircraft
POWERPLANT: 1 x 21,750 pounds (21,750 pounds) Rolls Royce Mk 105 Pegasus vectored-thrust turbofan
PERFORMANCE: maximum speed at sea level 661 mph (1065 km/h); service ceiling more than 50,000 feet (15,240 m); combat radius with 6000 pound (2722 kg) bombload 172 miles (277 km)
WEIGHTS: empty 15,542 pounds (7050 kg); maximum take-off 31,000 pounds (14,061 kg)
WINGSPAN: 30 feet 4 inches (9.25 m)
LENGTH: 47 feet 2 inches (14.36 m)
HEIGHT: 11 feet 8 inches (3.55 m)
WING AREA: 230 feet^2 (21.37 m^2)
ARMAMENT: 0.98 inches (2 x 25 mm) Aden cannon with 100 rpg; 6 x external hardpoints with provision for up to 9000 pounds (4082 kg) (short take-off) or 7000 pounds (3175 kg) (vertical take-off) of stores, including AAMs, ASMs, freefall or guided bombs, cluster bombs, dispenser weapons, napalm tanks, rocket launchers and ECM pods

Boeing B-52D Stratofortress

The B-52 has been in continuous service with Strategic Air Command in one form or another since 1955, with service life for the current generation of B- 52H aircraft likely to continue well into the 2040s. Development of this remarkable warhorse, which started life as a turboprop-powered project, began in 1945. The first prototype flew on October 2, 1951 and deliveries of 98 A, B and C models began in June 1955. Boeing extensively revised the fore-control system for the tail-mounted armament of four 12.7 mm machine guns for the B-52D (Model 464-201-7). The company built 101 B-52Ds at its Seattle plant, before production was moved to Wichita where another 69 were completed. Deliveries of this version began in 1956. The aircraft had been designed to carry stand-off nuclear weapons, but in 1964 a rebuilding program began to allow it to carry 105 "iron bombs".

SPECIFICATIONS

COUNTRY OF ORIGIN: United States
TYPE: long-range strategic bomber
POWERPLANT: 8 x 10,000 pounds (4536 kg) Pratt & Whitney J57 turbojets
PERFORMANCE: maximum speed at 24,000 feet (7315 m) 630 mph (1014 km/h): service ceiling 45,000 feet-55,000 feet (13,720m-16,765 m); standard range with maximum load 6,200 miles (9978 km)
WEIGHTS: empty 171,000–193,000 pounds (77,200–87,100 kg); loaded 450,000 pounds (204,120 kg)
WINGSPAN: 185 feet (56.4 m)
LENGTH: 157 feet 7 inches (48 m)
HEIGHT: 48 feet 3 inches (14.75 m)
WING AREA: 4000 feet^2 (371.60 m^2)
ARMAMENT: remotely controlled tail mounting with 4 x 12.7 mm machine guns; normal internal bomb capacity 27,000 pounds (12,247 kg) including all SAC special weapons; modified to take up to 70,000 pounds (31,750 kg) of conventional bombs on internal and external pylons

Boeing P-8 Poseidon

The P-8 Poseidon was conceived as a replacement for the ageing P-3 Orion maritime surveillance aircraft. It is based on the commercial Boeing 737 airframe, but, unlike previous conversions, military modifications are built in as the aircraft is constructed rather than being added after completion. The P-8 is a multi-mission platform, capable of attacking a range of surface and submarine targets and gathering electronic intelligence in addition to its reconnaissance role. It is designed to operate with unmanned air vehicles (UAVs) to allow wider coverage. As with many recent platforms, emphasis was placed on interoperability and information sharing to maximize the efficiency of all platforms involved in a mission. Thus the Poseidon can make an attack with missiles or anti-submarine weapons, or can hand off targeting data to another platform (ship, aircraft, or submarine) in the vicinity.

SPECIFICATIONS

COUNTRY OF ORIGIN: United States
TYPE: twin-engined maritime patrol aircraft
POWERPLANT: 27,000 lbf (2 x 120 kN) CFM International CFM56-7 engines
PERFORMANCE: maximum speed 490 mph (789 kph); ceiling 12,000 feet (12,496 m); range 1380 miles (2222 km)
WEIGHTS: empty 138,300 pounds (62,730 kg); maximum take-off 187,699 pounds (85,139 kg)
WINGSPAN: 123 feet 6 inches (37.64 m)
LENGTH: 129 feet 5 inches (39.47 m)
HEIGHT: 42 feet 1 inch (12.83 m)
ARMAMENT: 4 x wing and 2 x centerline pylons plus 5 x internal stations for missiles, torpedoes and naval mines

Cessna A-37B Dragonfly

The 318E is a development of the Cessna Model T-37, one of the jet aircraft used during the 1950s and 1960s for pilot training in the US. In 1962, two T-37s were evaluated by the USAFs Special Warfare Center for possible use in the counterinsurgency role. The aircraft were subsequently modified to accept engines that produced more than double the power of the original Continental J69-T-25s, permitting an increase in the possible weapons load. The war in Southeast Asia highlighted the need for such an aircraft and Cessna were requested in 1966 to convert 39 T-37s from the production line to a light strike role, equipped with eight underwing hardpoints, wing tip tanks, and powered by the more powerful engines. Delivery began in May 1967. The A-37B had a reinforced structure, increased maximum fuel capacity, and provision for inflight refueling.

SPECIFICATIONS

COUNTRY OF ORIGIN: United States
TYPE: light attack and reconnaissance aircraft
POWERPLANT: 2 x 2850 pounds (1293 kg) General Electric J85-GE-17A turbojets
PERFORMANCE: maximum speed at 16,000 feet (4875 m) 507 mph (816 km/h); service ceiling 41,765 feet (12,730 m); range with 4100 pounds (1860 kg) load 460 miles (740 km)
WEIGHTS: empty 6211 pounds (2817 kg); maximum take-off 14,000 pounds (6350 kg)
WINGSPAN: (over tip tanks) 35 feet 10.25 in (10.93 m)
LENGTH: 28 feet 3 inches (8.62 m)
HEIGHT: 8 feet 10 inches (2.7 m)
WING AREA: 183.9 feet^2 (17.09 m^2)
ARMAMENT: 1 x 7.62 mm GAU-2 Minigun six-barrell machine gun, 8 x underwing hardpoints with provision for more than 5000 pounds (2268 kg) of stores, including bombs, rocket and gun pods, napalm tanks, and other equipment

Dassault Super Etendard

During the late 1960s, it had been expected that the original Etendard force would be replaced in about 1971 by a specially developed carrier version of the Jaguar. This was rejected by the Aeronavale for political and financial reasons and Dassault's proposal for an improved Etendard was chosen. The new aircraft has a substantially redesigned structure, a more efficient engine, inertial navigation system, and other upgraded avionics. The first prototype flew on October 3, 1975; deliveries to the Aeronavale began in June, 1978. Fourteen Super Etendards were supplied to Argentina from November, 1981; the five which had been delivered by the following spring were used to great effect against British shipping during the Falklands War.

SPECIFICATIONS

COUNTRY OF ORIGIN: France

TYPE: single-seat carrierborne strike/attack and interceptor aircraft

POWERPLANT: 1 x 11,023 pounds (5000 kg) SNECMA Atar 8K-50 turbojet

PERFORMANCE: maximum speed 733 mph (1180 km/h) at low level; service ceiling 44,950 feet (13,700 m); combat radius 528 miles (850 km) on hi-lo-hi mission with one Exocet and two external tanks

WEIGHTS: empty 14,330 pounds (6500 kg); maximum take-off 26,455 pounds (12,000 kg)

WINGSPAN: 31 feet 6 in (9.6m)

LENGTH: 47 feet (14.31 m)

HEIGHT: 12 feet 8 inches (3.86 m)

WING AREA: 305.7 feet^2 (28.4 m^2)

ARMAMENT: 2 x 30 mm DEFA 553 cannon with 125 rpg, 5 x external hardpoints with provision for up to 4630 pounds (2100 kg) of stores, including nuclear weapons, Exocet and (Argentina only) Martin Pescador air-to-surface missiles, Magic air-to-air missiles, bombs and rockets, refueling and reconnaissance pods

Douglas B-66 Destroyer

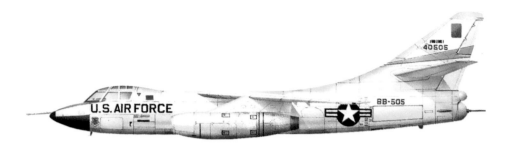

The B-66 Destroyer was produced by Douglas at Long Beach to meet the needs of the US Air Force, whose involvement in the Korean war had highlighted an urgent need for a high performance tactical bomber. Air Force chiefs planned to speed the availability of such an aircraft by procuring a modified version of the A-3D then in service with the US Navy. However, what began as a minimal modification of the A-3 turned into a totally different aircraft. Though it looked similar, hardly a single airframe part or item of equipment was common and the B-66 proved difficult to maintain and expensive. The arrestor gear, folding wing and tail mechanisms, plus the strengthened gear were all junked in favor of crew ejector seats, multiple camera installation, and precision bombing and navigation radar. Many were built as Elint and ECM aircraft and saw action over Southeast Asia.

SPECIFICATIONS

COUNTRY OF ORIGIN: United States
TYPE: all-day/night reconnaissance and bombing aircraft
POWERPLANT: 2 x 10,200 pounds (4627 kg) Allison J71-A-11 turbojets
PERFORMANCE: maximum speed 631mph (1015 km/h); service ceiling 38,900 feet (11,855 m); combat radius 925 miles (1489 km)
WEIGHTS: empty 43,476 pounds (19,720 kg); maximum take-off 83,000 pounds (37,648 kg)
WINGSPAN: 72 feet 6 inches (22.1 m)
LENGTH: 75 feet 2 inches (22.9 m)
HEIGHT: 23 feet 7 inches (7.19 m)
WING AREA: 780 feet^2 (72.46 m^2)
ARMAMENT: 2 x remotely controlled 20 mm cannon in tail turret, plus provision for 12,000 pounds (5443 kg) of conventional or nuclear weapons in internal bomb bay

Embraer R-99/E-99

The R-99 was developed from a civilian light airliner, the ERJ 145. Modifications included improved engines along with a reinforced airframe and advanced flight electronics. Primarily an airborne early warning (AEW) and air traffic control platform, the R-99 can also be used for patrol work such as border security operations. The R-99 is much smaller and cheaper than previous AEW aircraft and reportedly not much less capable; it can detect a fighter-sized target at a reported range of 217 miles (350 km) or more. As with many modern platforms, the aircraft's systems are designed to interface with ground stations and other platforms in real-time, enabling fast sharing of information. A maritime patrol version, designated P-99, is available, along with an Airborne Remote Sensing version with a different equipment fit. This aircraft, designated EMB-145 RS (illustrated above), is designed for electronic intelligence gathering.

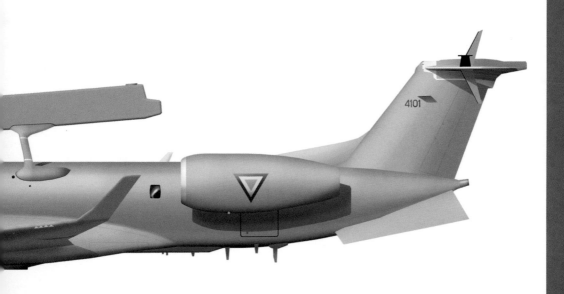

SPECIFICATIONS

COUNTRY OF ORIGIN: Brazil
TYPE: twin-engined patrol aircraft
POWERPLANT: 2 x 7426 pounds (3368 kg) thrust
Allison AE3007A turbofans
PERFORMANCE: maximum speed (in excess of) 518
mph (834 kph); ceiling 37,000 feet (11,277 m); range
1876 miles (3019 km)
WEIGHTS: empty 25,882 pounds (11,740
kg); maximum take-off 46517.5 pounds
(21,100 kg)
WINGSPAN: 65 feet 9 inches (20.04 m)
LENGTH: 93 feet 4 inches (28.45 m)
HEIGHT: 22 feet 2 inches (6.76 m)

Embraer Super Tucano

The Super Tucano, which first flew in 1992, is based on the successful and widely exported Tucano trainer. It is faster and can operate at a higher altitude, and can function as an advanced trainer in addition to its patrol, counter-insurgency, and light strike applications. The cockpit makes use of multifunction displays and an integrated weapons management system, which records data for post-mission analysis. The pilot is protected by Kevlar armor and equipped with an ejector seat. For strike missions, the Super Tucano has five hardpoints capable of mounting gun pods, bombs, and short-range air-to-air and air-to-ground missiles. A two-seat version, designated AT-29, is available. It mounts a thermal imaging system for night operations. The Super Tucano has achieved modest export success within Latin America, where it is often used for border patrol and anti-drug operations.

SPECIFICATIONS

COUNTRY OF ORIGIN: Brazil
TYPE: single or two-seat piston-engined trainer/light strike aircraft
POWERPLANT: 1 x 1299 hp (969 kW) Pratt & Whitney Canada PT6A-68A turboprop engine
PERFORMANCE: maximum speed 347.8 mph (560 kph); ceiling 35,006 feet (10,670 m); range over 931.6 miles (1500 km)
WEIGHTS: empty 5335 pounds (2420 kg); maximum take-off 11,464 pounds (5200 kg)
WINGSPAN: 37 feet 7 inches (11.14 m)
LENGTH: 37 feet 5 inches (11.42 m)
HEIGHT: 12 feet 10 inches (3.9 m)
ARMAMENT: 2 x wing-mounted (12.7 mm) machineguns; 5 x hardpoints for 3307 pounds (1500 kg) of additional stores

Fairchild A-10A Thunderbolt II

The Fairchild Republic A-10A grew out of the US Air Force's A-X program, which begun in 1967, to produce a highly battleproof, heavily-armed close air support aircraft to replace the A-1 Skyraider. In December, 1970, three companies were chosen to build prototypes for evaluation and Fairchild's YA-10A emerged as the winner in January, 1973. Six pre-production aircraft were submitted for evaluation, resulting in a production contract for 52A-10As in December, 1974. Some 727 have been procured by the USAF. The A-10A is dominated by the huge GAU-8/A cannon, but the range of weaponry that it can carry is truly devastating. This was proved effectively during actions against Iraqi armor in the 1991 Persian Gulf War, although critics have questioned whether its slow speed would make it more vulnerable against a more formidable enemy.

SPECIFICATIONS

COUNTRY OF ORIGIN: United States
TYPE: single-seat close support aircraft
POWERPLANT: 2 x 9065 pounds (4112 kg) General Electric TF34-GE-100 turbofans
PERFORMANCE: maximum speed at sea level 439 mph (706 km/h); combat radius 250 miles (402 km) for a 2-hour loiter with 18 Mk82 bombs plus 750 rounds cannon a mmunition
WEIGHTS: empty 24,959 pounds (11,321 kg); maximum take-off 50,000 pounds (22,680 kg)
WINGSPAN: 57 feet 6 inches (17.53 m)
LENGTH: 53 feet 4 inches (16.26 m)
HEIGHT: 14 feet 8 inches (4.47 m)
WING AREA: 506 feet^2 (47.01m^2)
ARMAMENT: 1.18 inches (1 x 30 mm) GAU-8/A rotary cannon with capacity for 1350 rounds of a mmunition, 11 x hardpoints with provision for up to 16,000 pounds (7528 kg) of disposable stores; weapons include conventional bombs, incendiary bombs, Rockeye cluster bombs, AGM-65 Maverick air-to-surface missiles, laser and optronically guided bombs and SUU-23 20 mm cannon pods

General Atomics MQ-9 Reaper

The Reaper began life as "Predator B", a larger and more capable version of the Predator unmanned air vehicle (UAV), commonly known as a drone. It can be controlled from the same ground station, but shares few components with its predecessor. The Reaper was designed to carry out long range or high-endurance surveillance and reconnaissance missions, but can be armed with Stinger or Hellfire missiles or GPS-guided bombs for the strike role. A maritime version, named Mariner, was created as a contender for the US Navy's Broad Area Maritime Surveillance UAV contract, but lost out to a Northrop-Grumman design. The navy version of Reaper has since attracted interest from Australia and the US Coast Guard, while standard Reapers are currently serving with US Homeland Security forces as well as the armed forces of Britain, Italy, Turkey, and Mexico.

SPECIFICATIONS

COUNTRY OF ORIGIN: Unitd States
TYPE: Remotely Piloted Vehicle (RPV)/Unmanned Air Vehicle (UAV)
POWERPLANT: 1 x 950 hp (709 kW) Honeywell TPE331-10T turboprop
PERFORMANCE: maximum speed 300 mph (482 kph); ceiling 50,000 feet (15,240 m); range over 3682 miles (5926 km)
WEIGHTS: empty 6000 pounds (2722 kg); maximum take-off 10,000 pounds (4536 kg)
WINGSPAN: 66 feet (20.12 m)
LENGTH: 36 feet (10.97 m)
HEIGHT: 12 feet 6 inches (3.6 m)
ARMAMENT: 7 x hardpoints for Hellfire or Stinger missiles, laser-guided or GPS-guided bombs

Grumman A-6 Intruder

Selected from 11 competing designs in December, 1957, the Intruder was specifically planned for first pass blind attack on-point surface targets at night or in any weather conditions. The aircraft was designed to be subsonic and is powered by two straight turbojets. In the original design, the efflux was routed through tilting jetpips to enhance STOL capabilities. Despite its considerable gross weight, the Intruder has excellent slow flying qualities with full span slats and flaps. The crew are afforded a good all-around view by the broad canopy. The navigator controls one of the most sophisticated avionics suites on any current aircraft. The Intruder first came into service with the US Navy in February 1963; during the Vietnam War the A-6A was worked round-the-clock on precision bombing missions that no other aircraft was capable of undertaking until the introduction of the F-111.

SPECIFICATIONS

COUNTRY OF ORIGIN: United States
TYPE: two-seat carrierborne and landbased all-weather strike aircraft
POWERPLANT: 2 x 9300 pounds (4218 kg) Pratt & Whitney J52-P-8A turbojets
PERFORMANCE: maximum speed at sea level 648 mph (1043 km/h); service ceiling 47,500 feet (14,480 m); range with full weapon load 1011 miles (1627 km)
WEIGHTS: empty 26,746 pounds (12,132 kg); maximum take-off 58,600 pounds (26,581 kg) for carrier launch or 60,400 pounds (27,397 kg) for field take-off
WINGSPAN: 53 feet (16.15 m)
LENGTH: 54 feet 9 inches (16.69 m)
HEIGHT: 16 feet 2 inches (4.93 m)
WING AREA: 528.9 feet^2 (49.13m^2)
ARMAMENT: 5 x external hardpoints with provision for up to 18,000 pounds (8165 kg) of stores, including nuclear weapons, conventional and guided bombs, air-to-surface missiles, and drop tanks

Grumman EA-6 Prowler

The US Navy rarely undertakes a strike mission without the protection offered by the EA-6 ECM. This aircraft was developed from the successful A-6 Intruder family, although it is substantially different in almost every respect. The large cockpit provides seating for the pilot and three electronic warfare officers, who control the most sophisticated and advanced ECM equipment ever fitted to a tactical aircraft. At the heart of this system is the ALQ-99 tactical jamming system, which is capable of dealing with multiple hostile electronic signals across a broad range of frequencies. The aircraft first entered service in 1972 with VAQ-132. Despite its proven capabilities, the Prowler was only produced in small numbers. In the mid-1990s, the US Navy updated many aircraft to ADVCAP (Advanced Capability Standard).

SPECIFICATIONS

COUNTRY OF ORIGIN: United States
TYPE: electronic countermeasures platform
POWERPLANT: 2 x 11,200 pounds (5080 kg) Pratt & Whitney J52-P-408 turbojets
PERFORMANCE: maximum speed at sea level 610 mph (982 km/h); service ceiling 38,000 feet (11,580 m); combat range with full external fuel 1769 km (1099 miles)
WEIGHTS: empty 32,162 pounds (14,588 kg); maximum take-off 65,000 pounds (29,484 kg)
WINGSPAN: 53 feet (16.15 m)
LENGTH: 59 feet 10 inches (18.24 m)
HEIGHT: 16 feet 3 inches (4.95 m)
WING AREA: 528.9 feet^2 (49.13 m^2)
ARMAMENT: none on early models, retrofitted with external hardpoints for 4 or 6 x AGM-88 HARM air-to-surface anti-radar missiles

Hawker P.1127

In the 1950s, the realization that the thrust/weight ratio of the gas turbine made possible a new class of high speed jets with VTOL (vertical takeoff and landing) capability led to a rash of unconventional prototypes and research machines. With the exception of the far less capable Yakovlev Yak-38 "Forger", only one has led to a useful combat aircraft. This was the P.1127, designed by a team led by Hawker chief designer Sir Sidney Camm around the unique Bristol BS.53, which had been designed specifically to provide jet-lift to vertical lift-off fixed wing aircraft. The engine was tested on a bizarre rig accurately nicknamed "The Flying Bedstead". The first of seven prototypes P.1127 made its initial hovering flight on October 21, 1960. Vertical takeoff was achieved by vectoring the thrust from the engine down through four adjustable nozzles, which could then be swivelled to make the transition to level flight.

SPECIFICATIONS

COUNTRY OF ORIGIN: United Kingom
TYPE: experimental V/STOL aircraft
POWERPLANT: (typical; many installations were used during trials of the 6 prototypes) 1 x 19,000 pounds (8618 kg) Rolls-Royce Pegasus vectoring thrust turbojet
PERFORMANCE: Mach 1.2 (in dive)

Ilyushin Il-28 "Beagle"

First appearing in prototype form as early as 1948, the Il-28 afforded Eastern Bloc armed forces the same degree of flexibility and duration of service as the Canberra did for the UK. The prototype was powered by two Soviet-built turbojets developed directly from the Rolls-Royce Nene, supplied by the UK government in a fit of contrition. The unswept wing is set high and well back on the fuselage, to reduce the movement caused by fuel tanks located in the rear fuselage and the aft gunners compartment. The gunner also acts as the radio operator, with the navigator housed in the glazed nose section. After a public flyby during the 1950 May Day parade, Soviet units began to equip with the Il-28. The aircraft served with all Warsaw Pact light bomber units between 1955–70. A trainer version (Il-28U) was also produced.

SPECIFICATIONS

COUNTRY OF ORIGIN: Soviet Union
TYPE: three-seat bomber and ground attack/dual control trainer/torpedo carrier
POWERPLANT: 2 x 5952 kg (2700 kg) Klimov VK-1 turbojets
PERFORMANCE: maximum speed 560 mph (902 km/h); service ceiling 40,355 feet (12,300 m); range 1355 miles (2180 km); with bomb load 684 miles (1100 km)
WEIGHTS: empty 28,418 pounds (12,890 kg); maximum take-off 46,738 pounds (21,200 kg)
WINGSPAN: 70 feet 5 inches (21.45 m)
LENGTH: 57 feet 11 inches (17.65 m)
HEIGHT: 22 feet (6.70 m)
WING AREA: 654.47 feet^2 (60.80 m^2)
ARMAMENT: 2 x 23 mm NR-23 fixed cannon in nose, 2 x 23 mm NR-23 trainable cannon in tail turret; internal bomb capacity of up to 2205 pounds (1000 kg), maximum bomb capacity 6614 pounds (3000 kg); torpedo version had provision for 2 x 400 mm light torpedoes

Kawasaki C-1

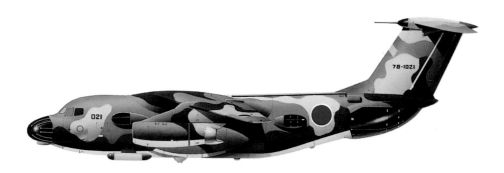

The C-1 was designed specifically to replace the fearsome Curtiss C-46 Commando transport aircraft in service with the Japanese Air Self Defense Force. The first two prototypes were built during 1968 by Kawasaki Heavy Industries from a design submitted by the Nihon Aeroplane Manufacturing Company. The first flight was made in November, 1970; flight testing and evaluation led to a production order for 11 in 1972. The C-1 follows conventional military transport design with a high set wing configuration to maximize cabin volume, podded main landing gear, and a rear loading ramp. Limited maximum payload curtailed plans to develop versions, with the exception of the sole C-1Kai ECM trainer pictured. This aircraft differs from standard models by distinctive radomes on the nose and tail, an ALQ-5 ECM system, and antennae beneath the fuselage.

SPECIFICATIONS

COUNTRY OF ORIGIN: Japan
TYPE: ECM trainer aircraft
POWERPLANT: 2 x 14,500 pounds (6577 kg) Mitsubishi (Pratt & Whitney) JT8-M-9 turbofans
PERFORMANCE: maximum speed at 25,000 feet (7620 m) 501 mph (806 km/h); service ceiling 38,000 feet (11,580 m); range 808 miles (1300 km) with 17,417 pounds (7900 kg) payload
WEIGHTS: empty 51,412 pounds (23320 kg); maximum take-off 99,208 pounds (45,000 kg)
WINGSPAN: 100 feet 5 inches (30.6 m)
LENGTH: 100 feet 4 inches (30.5 m)
HEIGHT: 32 feet 10 inches (10 m)
WING AREA: 1297.09 feet^2 (102.5 m^2)

Lockheed C-5A Galaxy

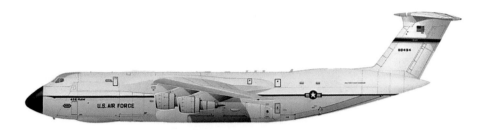

For a time during the early 1970s, the giant C-5 Galaxy reigned as the world's largest aircraft, although it has now been overtaken by the HAV 304 "Airlander" developed for the US Army. Despite its huge size, the Galaxy can operate from rough airstrips. To this end it has a high flotation landing gear with 28 wheels. During the development program, extreme difficulties were encountered with its aerodynamics and structural weight. As the result, the unit cost escalated and eventually production had to be cut to a total of 81, equipping four MAC squadrons. The aircraft can carry complete missile systems and M1 Abrams tanks to potential trouble spots around the globe and has proved an invaluable asset to the US armed forces in this role. In 1982 the C-5B was authorized. This included the modifications evolved in the C-5A — uprated engines, extended life wing, and better avionics.

SPECIFICATIONS

COUNTRY OF ORIGIN: United States
TYPE: heavy strategic transport
POWERPLANT: (C5A) 4 x 41,000 pounds (18,642 kg) General Electric TF39-1turbofans
PERFORMANCE: maximum speed 571 mph (919 km/h); service ceiling at 615,000 pounds (272,910 kg) 34,000 feet (10,360 m); range with maximum payload 220,967 pounds (100,228 kg) 3749 miles (6033 km)
WEIGHTS: empty 325,244 pounds (147,528 kg); maximum take-off 769,000 pounds (348,810 kg)
WINGSPAN: 222 feet 8 inches (67.88 m)
LENGTH: 247 feet 10 inches (75.54 m)
HEIGHT: 65 feet 2 inches (19.85 m)
WING AREA: 6200 feet^2 (575.98 m^2)

Lockheed Martin Super Hercules

The Super Hercules was developed by Lockheed as a private venture, first flying in April 1996 and entering service in January 1999. It has an advanced cockpit, which makes extensive use of multifunction displays and also incorporates a number of refinements that are intended to reduce maintenance time and personnel workload, resulting in significant savings across the lifetime of the aircraft. New, more powerful engines contribute to improved short-field performance and give a higher cruising speed and rate of climb. The C130J is one of the few military aircraft to mark more than 50 years of continuous service. The model has been widely exported and is in service with the US Marine Corps and Coast Guard as well as the Air Force. A special operations version is under development for use by special forces.

SPECIFICATIONS
COUNTRY OF ORIGIN: United States
TYPE: four-engined transport aircraft
POWERPLANT: 4 x 4591 hp (3425 kW) Allison AE 2100D3 turboprops
PERFORMANCE: maximum speed 403 mph (648 kph); ceiling 28,000 feet (8615 m); range 3279 miles (5247 km)
WEIGHTS: empty 75,562 pounds (34,274 kg); maximum take-off 175,000 pounds (79,379 kg)
WINGSPAN: 132 feet 7 inches (40.41 m)
LENGTH: 97 feet 9 inches (29.79 m)
HEIGHT: 38 feet 9 inches (11.81 m)

McDonnell Douglas A-4F Skyhawk

During its long service career the Skyhawk has proved to be one of the most versatile combat aircraft ever built, disproving those who argued that the small, lightweight machine would be outclassed by bigger, heavier aircraft. The aircraft pictured is an A-4F, which is distinguished by the dorsal hump carrying additional avionics and the J52-P-8A engine. It bears the markings of Attack Squadron 212, Carrier Air Wing 21, and has the registration of the Air Wing Commander. While equipped with this model, VAF-212 deployed four times to the Gulf of Tonkin aboard USS *Hancock*. The aircraft is loaded with a typical mixture external stores, including 500 pounds (227 kg) Mk 82 bombs, two 300 gallon (1321 litre) drop tanks and two AGM-12 Bullpup-A ASMs. One hundred aircraft were refitted with the 11,000 pounds (4990 kg) J52-P-401.

SPECIFICATIONS

COUNTRY OF ORIGIN: United States
TYPE: single-seat attack bomber
POWERPLANT: 1 x 9300 pounds (4218 kg) J52-8A turbojet
PERFORMANCE: maximum speed 670 mph (1078 km/h); service ceiling 49,000 feet (14,935 m); range with 4000 pound load 920 miles (1480 km)
WEIGHTS: empty 10,602 pounds (4809 kg); maximum take-off 27,420 pounds (12,437 kg)
WINGSPAN: 27 feet 6 inches (8.38 m)
LENGTH: excluding probe 40 feet 1 inch (12.22 m)
HEIGHT: 15 feet 3 inches (4.66 m)
WING AREA: 260 feet^2 (24.15 m^2)
ARMAMENT: 2 x 20 mm Mk 12 cannon with 200 rpg; 5 x external hardpoints with provision for 8200 pounds (3720 kg) of stores including AGM-12 Bullpup air-to-surface missiles, AGM-45 Shrike anti-radar missiles, bombs, cluster bombs, dispenser weapons, rocket-launcher pods, cannon pods, drop tanks, and ECM pods

MD CF-17A Globemaster III

After a difficult development program, the Globemaster III now occupies a position as one of the finest heavy-lift transport aircraft in current service. The early problems encountered during development have been ironed out and the aircraft can look forward to a long service life with MAC. The aircraft was designed and developed during the early 1980s to replace the C-141 Starlifter fleet. Cabin volume is similar to the much larger C-5 Galaxy, coupled with the short-field capability of the C-130 Hercules. Service deliveries began in 1994 and confidence in the aircraft's abilities have grown steadily. Although technically a highly complex aircraft, maintenance hours per flying hour are impressively low. They are also flown by the airforces in the UK, Australia, and India.

SPECIFICATIONS

COUNTRY OF ORIGIN: United States
TYPE: heavy strategic transport
POWERPLANT: 4 x 41,700 pounds (18,195 kg) Pratt & Whitney F117-P-100 turbofans
PERFORMANCE: maximum cruising speed at 35,000 feet (10,670 m) 515 mph (829 km/h); service ceiling 45,000 feet (13,715 m); range with 124,000 pounds (56,245 kg); payload 3225 miles (5190 km)
WEIGHTS: empty 269,000 pounds (122,016 kg); maximum take-off 580,000 pounds (263,083 kg)
WINGSPAN: 165 feet (50.29 m)
LENGTH: 174 feet (53.04 m)
HEIGHT: 55 feet 1 inch (16.79 m)
WING AREA: 3800 feet^2 (353 m^2)

Mikoyan-Gurevich MiG-27

The MiG-27 was a highly developed version of the MiG-23. The aircraft was designed from the outset as a dedicated ground attack aircraft and is optimized for operations over the battlefield. The most obvious difference is the nose, which was designed to give the pilot an enhanced view of the ground during approaches. Because it was only necessary to house a laser rangefinder and marked-target seeker in the nose, it was possible for the MiG designers to taper the nose steeply, as can be seen above. The pilot is protected from small-arms fire by armor plating on the side of the cockpit and to enhance low-level performance, the variable geometry inlets and variable nozzle are replaced by lighter fixed units. The aircraft began to enter service in the late 1970s.

SPECIFICATIONS

COUNTRY OF ORIGIN: Soviet Union
TYPE: single-seat ground attack aircraft
POWERPLANT: 1 x 23,353 pounds (11,500 kg) Tumanskii R-29B-300 turbojet
PERFORMANCE: maximum speed at 26,250 feet (8000 m) 1170 mph (1885 km/h); service ceiling over 45,900 feet (14,000 m); combat radius on lo-lo-lo mission with full weapon load and three tanks 335 miles (540 km)
WEIGHTS: empty 26,252 pounds (11,908 kg); maximum loaded 44,750 pounds (20,300 kg)
WINGSPAN: 45 feet 10 inches (13.97 m) spread and 25 feet 6 inches (7.78 m) swept
LENGTH: 56 feet (17.07 m)
HEIGHT: 16 feet 5 inches (5 m)
WING AREA: 402 feet^2 (37.35m^2) spread
ARMAMENT: 1 x 23 mm GSh-23L cannon with 200 rounds, 7 x external hardpoints with provision for up to 8818 pounds (4000 kg) of stores, Kh-29 air-to-surface missiles, AS-7 Kerry air-to-surface missiles, cannon pods, rocket launcher pods, large calibre rockets, napalm tanks, drop tanks, ECM pods, conventional and guided bombs

Mitsubishi F-1

Japan followed a somewhat unusual, but ultimately far-sighted route by developing the T-2 jet trainer before the F-1. Following the successful development of the T-2 Mitsubishi converted the second and third prototypes to single seat configuration, with the aim of producing a close-support fighter version. The first flight took place in 1975 and, after evaluation by the JASDF Air Proving Wing at Gifu, the aircraft was ordered into full time production. A total of 77 F-1S were ordered with deliveries commencing in September 1977. The final aircraft was received in March 1987, replacing the aging North American F-86 Sabres then in service. This particular aircraft served with the 3rd Air Squadron of the 3rd Air Wing of the Japanese Air Self Defense Force (JASDF) at Misawa in the early 1980s.

SPECIFICATIONS

COUNTRY OF ORIGIN: Japan
TYPE: close-support and anti-ship attack fighter
POWERPLANT: 2 x 7308 pounds (3315 kg) Ishikawajima-Harima TF40-IHI-801A turbofans
PERFORMANCE: maximum speed at 35,000 feet (10,675 m) 1,061 mph (1708 km/h); service ceiling 50,000 feet (15,240 m); combat radius on hi-lo-hi mission with 4,000 pounds (1816 kg) load 218 miles (350 km)
WEIGHTS: empty 14,017 pounds (6358 kg); maximum take-off 30,203 pounds (13,700 kg)
WINGSPAN: 25 feet 10 inches (7.88 m)
LENGTH: 58 feet 7 inches (17.86 m)
HEIGHT: 14 feet 5 inches (4.39 m)
WING AREA: 227.88 feet^2 (21.17 m^2)
ARMAMENT: 0.79 inches (1 x 20 mm) JM61Vulcan six-barrell cannon with 750 rounds, 5 x external hardpoints with provision for 6000 pounds (2722 kg) of stores, including air-to-surface missiles, conventional and guided bombs, rocket-launcher pods, drop tanks, ECM pods; two wingtip pylons for air-to-air missiles

Nanchang Q-5 "Fantan"

The basic design of the Fantan close-support fighter was derived from the Soviet Mikoyan-Gurevich MiG-19. Design of the aircraft began in 1958, which retains a similar wing and rear fuselage configuration. Power is provided by two turbojets mounted side-by-side in the fuselage, with an attack radar mounted in the nose. Service deliveries began in 1970 and, by 1980, approximately 100 were in service. Export customers have included Pakistan (52 A-5C), Bangladesh (20 A-5C), and North Korea (Q-5 IA). At one time, more than 900 of the aircraft served with the People's Liberation Army, Air Force, and Navy. The Nanchang factory, based in Kiangsi province, has also developed a modernized version of the basic model pictured equipped with an Alenia FIAR Pointer 2500 ranging radar for export. This is designated A-5M.

SPECIFICATIONS

COUNTRY OF ORIGIN: China
TYPE: single-seat close support fighter with secondary air combat capability
POWERPLANT: 7165 pounds (2 x 3250 kg) Shenyang WP-6 turbojets
PERFORMANCE: maximum speed at 36,090 feet (11,000 m) 739 mph (1190 km/h); service ceiling 52,500 feet (16,000 m); combat radius on low level mission with maximum load 249 miles (400 km)
WEIGHTS: empty 14,054 pounds (6375 kg); maximum take-off 26,080 pounds (11,830 kg)
WINGSPAN: 31 feet 9 inches (9.68 m)
LENGTH: including probe 51 feet 4 inches (15.65 m)
HEIGHT: 14 feet 3 inches (4.33 m)
WING AREA: 300.85 feet^2 (27.95 m^2)
ARMAMENT: 2 x 23 mm Type 23-2K cannon with 100 rpg; 10 x external hardpoints with provision for up to 4409 pounds (2000 kg) of stores, including air-toair missiles, fee-fall bombs, rocket launcher pods, napalm tanks, drop tanks, and ECM pods

Northrop Grumman RQ-4

Global Hawk was designed in the early 1990s to meet a USAF requirement for a long-range, high-altitude reconnaissance UAV. It first flew in 1998 and began operations over Afghanistan in 2001. Deployments to Iraq began in 2003. Production began before development was fully complete, and experience with early models led to a redesign of the wings and front fuselage. These changes were implemented on Global Hawks built after August 2006. The Global Hawk UAV is not armed, serving in a purely information-gathering role for which it uses synthetic aperture radar in addition to electro-optical systems. Its mission endurance is considerable; in 2001 a Global Hawk flew non-stop from the US to Australia to complete the first Pacific crossing by an unmanned aircraft. The RPV has attracted considerable international interest for military and scientific purposes, including exploration of remote areas.

SPECIFICATIONS

COUNTRY OF ORIGIN: United States
TYPE: Remotely Piloted Vehicle (RPV)/Unmanned Air Vehicle (UAV)
POWERPLANT: 1 x 7,050 lbf (31 kN) Allison/Rolls-Royce AE3007H turbofan
PERFORMANCE: maximum speed 400 mph (644 kph); ceiling 65,000 feet (19,812 m); range 15,525 miles (24,984 km)
WEIGHTS: empty 9200 pounds (4173 kg) maximum take-off 25,600 pounds (11,612 kg)
WINGSPAN: 116 feet 3 inches (35.43 m)
LENGTH: 44 feet (13.41 m)
HEIGHT: 15 feet 3 inches (4.63 m)

Northrop-Grumman B-2 Spirit

The B-2 has been developed from 1978 to a US Air Force requirement for a strategic penetration bomber to complement and replace the Rockwell B-1 Lancer and the Boeing B-52 Stratofortress. The aircraft was designed to incorporate low-observables (stealth technology), with Northrop as the prime contractor. The characteristic flying-wing stems from the extensive research carried out by the company in the 1950s. The B-2s radar reflectivity is very low because of smooth blended surfaces and the use of radiation-absorbent materials. Careful mixing of hot exhaust gases with cold airstream air reduces thermal and acoustic signals to a very significant extent. The original production order was cut from 132 to approximately 20 aircraft, both because of the enormous unit costs (over $1 billion) and due to the reduced threat from the former Soviet Union.

SPECIFICATIONS

COUNTRY OF ORIGIN: United States
TYPE: strategic bomber and missile-launch platform
POWERPLANT: 4 x 19,000 pounds (8618 kg) General Electric F118-GE-110 turbofans
PERFORMANCE: maximum speed at high altitude 475 mph (764 km/h); service ceiling 50,000 feet (15,240 m); range on high level mission with standard fuel and 37,300 pounds (16,919 kg) warload 7255 miles (11,675 km)
WEIGHTS: empty 100,000 pounds (45,360 kg); maximum take-off 400,000 pounds (181,437 kg)
WINGSPAN: 172 feet (52.43 m)
LENGTH: 69 feet (21.03 m)
HEIGHT: 17 feet (5.18 m)
WING AREA: more than 5000 feet^2 (464.50m^2)
ARMAMENT: 2 x internal bomb bays with provision for up to 50,000 pounds (22,680 kg) of stores; each bay can carry 1 x eight-round Boeing Rotary launcher for a total of 16 x 1.1 megaton B83 thermonuclear free-fall bombs, 22 x 1500 pounds (680 kg) bombs, or 80 x 500 pounds (227 kg) free-fall bombs

Panavia Tornado GR.Mk 1A

Germany and Italy provided the driving force for development of a centerline reconnaissance system that could be fitted to the Tornado Gr.Mk 1 and such a device was developed by Messerschmitt-Bolkow-Blohm in the early 1980s. The UK began flight trials with a GR.Mk 1, equipped with a reconnaissance pack fitted in the cannon ammunition bay in 1985. The pack contains infrared cameras, linescan, and thermal imaging modules, which conforms with a reconnaissance management system. These aircraft are designated GR.Mk 1A. They are readily identifiable by the small underbelly blister fairing and transparent side panels for the sideways-looking surveillance equipment. Deliveries of newbuilt aircraft to UK-based squadrons began in January 1990.

SPECIFICATIONS

COUNTRY OF ORIGIN: Germany, Italy, and UK
TYPE: all-weather day/night reconnaissance aircraft
POWERPLANT: 2 x 16,075 pounds (7292 kg) Turbo-Union RB.199-34R Mk 103 turbofans
PERFORMANCE: maximum speed above 36,090 feet (11,000 m) 1,452 mph (2337 km/h); service ceiling 50,000 feet (15,240 m); combat radius with weapon load on hi-lo-hi mission 864 miles (1390 km)
WEIGHTS: empty 31,065 pounds (14,091 kg); maximum take-off 60,000 pounds (27,216 kg)
WINGSPAN: 45 feet 8 inches (13.91 m) spread and 28 feet 3 inches (8.6 m) swept
LENGTH: 54 feet 10 inches (16.72 m)
HEIGHT: 19 feet 6 inches (5.95 m)
WING AREA: 286.3 feet^2 (26.6m^2)
ARMAMENT: 7 x external hardpoints with provision for up to 19,840 pounds (9000 kg) of stores, including nuclear weapons, JP233 runway denial weapon, ALARM anti-radiation missiles, air-to-air missiles, air-to-surface missiles, anti-ship missiles, conventional and guided bombs, cluster bombs, ECM pods and drop tanks

Republic F-105B Thunderchief

Even before the F-84F Thunderstreak had entered service, Republic had begun studies on an aircraft that it was hoped would replace it in service. The primary mission of this new aircraft was perceived as the delivery of nuclear and conventional weapons in all weather at high speeds and over long ranges. Contracts for two prototype aircraft were issued in 1954; the first flight was made in October 1955. No F105A production aircraft were built because of the availability of a more powerful powerplant and the company subsequently built four YF-105B aircraft with these engines. The production F-105B entered service in August 1958 with the USAF's 335th Tactical Fighter Squadron, three years later than planned. Seventy-five were completed before the aircraft was superseded by the F-105D.

SPECIFICATIONS

COUNTRY OF ORIGIN: United States
TYPE: single-seat fighter-bomber
POWERPLANT: 1 x 23,500 pounds (10,660 kg) Pratt & Whitney J75 turbojet
PERFORMANCE: maximum speed 1254 mph (2018 km/h); service ceiling 52,000 feet (15,850 m); combat radius with weapon load 230 miles (370 km)
WEIGHTS: empty 27,500 pounds (12,474 kg); maximum take-off 40,000 pounds (18,144 kg)
WINGSPAN: 34 feet 11 inches (10.65 m)
LENGTH: 64 feet 3 inches (19.58 m)
HEIGHT: 19 feet 8 inches (5.99 m)
WING AREA: 385 feet^2 (35.8 m^2)
ARMAMENT: 1 x 20 mm M61 cannon with 1029 rounds; internal bay with provision for up to 8000 pounds (3629 kg) of bombs; 5 x external pylons for additional load of 6000 pounds (2722 kg)

SEPECAT Jaguar A

Developed jointly by BAC in the UK and Dassault-Breguet in France (Societé Européenne de Production de l'Avion Ecole de Combat at Appui Tactique), to meet a joint requirement of the Armée de l'Air and UK Air Force, the Jaguar emerged from protracted development as a far more powerful and effective aircraft than originally envisioned. The original idea was for a light trainer and close-support machine with a 1300 pounds (590 kg) load, but with British pressure, this was considerably upgraded. Power was provided by a turbofan developed jointly from the Rolls-Royce RB.172 by Rolls Royce and Turbomeca. The first French version to fly was the two-seat E, followed in March 1969 by the Jaguar A single-seat tactical support aircraft, which form the backbone of the French tactical nuclear strike force. Service deliveries began in 1973, with production of some 160 aircraft.

SPECIFICATIONS

COUNTRY OF ORIGIN: France and UK
TYPE: single-seat tactical support and strike aircraft
POWERPLANT: 2 x 7305 pounds (3313 kg) Rolls-Royce/Turbomeca Adour Mk 102 turbofans
PERFORMANCE: maximum speed at 36,090 feet (11,000 m) 990 mph (1593 km/h); combat radius on lo-lo-lo mission with internal fuel 357 miles (557 km)
WEIGHTS: empty 15,432 pounds (7000 kg); maximum take-off 34,172 pounds (15,500 kg)
WINGSPAN: 28 feet 6 inches (8.69 m)
LENGTH: 55 feet 3 inchesx (55 feet 3 inches)
HEIGHT: 16 feet 1 inch (4.89 m)
WING AREA: 258.34 feet^2 (24 m^2)
ARMAMENT: 2 x 30 mm DEFA cannon with 150 rpg; 5 x external hardpoints with provision for 10,000 pounds (4536 kg) of stores, including 1 x AN-52 tactical nuclear weapon or conventional loads such as 1 x AS.37 Martel anti-radar missile and 2 x drop tanks, or 8 x 1000 pounds (454 kg) bombs, or combinations of ASMs, drop tanks and rocket launcher pods, and a reconnaissance pod

Sukhoi Su-20 "Fitter-C"

The first version of the variable-geometry wing Sukhoi Su-17 ground-attack aircraft made available for export was designated Su-20. This aircraft was basically similar to the Su-17M "Fitter C", with inboard wing fences, broader-cord tailfin, and a single brake parachute, plus eight stores pylons. Poland was the only country to receive the full-standard "Fitter-C", but a reduced equipment version was operated by Afghanistan, Algeria, Angola, Egypt, Iraq, North Korea, and Vietnam. A later version, designated Su-22, was also produced, with an undernose pod housing terrain-avoidance radar and pulse-Doppler radar. Another feature that distinguishes the Su-22 from the Su-20, with its constant section rear fuselage, is the distinct bulge a feet of the main wheels. This structural change was necessary to accommodate the Khachaturov turbojet, which replaces the Lyul'ka unit on the Su-20.

SPECIFICATIONS

COUNTRY OF ORIGIN: Soviet Union
TYPE: single-seat ground attack fighter
POWERPLANT: 1 x 24,802 pounds (11,250 kg) Lyul'ka AL-21F-3 turbojet
PERFORMANCE: maximum speed above 36,090 feet (11,000 m) approximately 1380 mph (2220 km/h); service ceiling 49,865 feet (15,200 m); combat radius on hilo- hi mission with 4409 pounds (2000 kg) load 419 miles (675 km)
WEIGHTS: empty 20,944 pounds (9,500 kg); maximum take-off 42,990 pounds (19,500 kg)
WINGSPAN: 45 feet 3 inches (13.80 m) spread and 32 feet 10 inches (10 m) swept;
LENGTH: 61 feet 6 inches (18.75 m)
HEIGHT: 16 feet 5 inches (5 m)
WING AREA: 430 feet^2 (40 m^2)
ARMAMENT: 2 x 30 mm NR-30 cannon with 80 rpg; 9 x external pylons with provision for up to 9370 pounds (4250 kg) of stores, including tactical nuclear weapons, air-to-air missiles, air-to-surface missiles, guided bombs, cluster bombs, dispenser weapons, napalm tanks, large caliber rockets, rocket-launcher pods, cannon pods, drop tanks and ECM pods

Sukhoi Su-25 "Frogfoot-A"

Western intelligence sources first identified the "Frogfoot" at Ramenskoye test center in 1977 and gave it the provisional US designation "Ram-J". The prototype first flew in 1975 and production of the single-seat close-support Su-25K (often compared to the Fairchild A-10 Thunderbolt II) began in 1978. The pilot sits in an armored cockpit and, on the Su-25K, had a Sirena-3 radar-warning system and tailcone mounted chaff/decoy flare dispenser to protect his aircraft. A nose-mounted laser range finder and marked target seeker reportedly allows bombing accuracy to within 16 feet 5 inches (5 m) over a stand-off range of 12.5 miles (20 km). A trial unit was deployed to Afghanistan as early as 1980, followed by a full squadron, to support Soviet troops fighting in the mountainous country. The squadron worked closely with Mi-24 "Hind" gunships and the aircraft became fully operational in 1984.

SPECIFICATIONS

COUNTRY OF ORIGIN: Soviet Union
TYPE: single-seat close-support aircraft
POWERPLANT: 2 x 4500 kg (9921 pounds) Tumanskii R-195 turbojets
PERFORMANCE: maximum speed at sea level 606 mph (975 km/h); service ceiling 7000 m (22,965 feet); combat radius on lo-lo-lo mission with 9700 pounds (4400 kg) load 466 miles (750 km)
WEIGHTS: empty 20,950 pounds (9,500 kg); maximum take-off 17,600 kg (38,800 pounds)
WINGSPAN: 47 feet 2 inches (14.36 m)
WINGAREA: 362.75 feet^2 (33.7 m^2)
LENGTH: 51 feet (15.53 m)
HEIGHT: 15 feet 9 inches (4.8 m)
ARMAMENT: 1 x 30 mm GSh-30-2 cannon with 250 rds; 8 x external pylons with provision for up to 9700 pounds (4400 kg) of stores, including AAMs, ASMs, ARMs, anti-tank missiles, guided bombs, cluster bombs, dispenser weapons, large-calibre rockets, rocket-launcher pods, drop tanks and ECM pods

Tupolev Tu-22M "Backfire-A"

The Tu-22M "Backfire" began life as a swing-wing derivative of the Tu-22 "Blinder" supersonic bomber and maritime patrol aircraft. The inability of this aircraft to fly strategic missions to the US (because of short range) led the Tupolev bureau to produce the "Backfire-A" prototype (designated Tu-22M). Evaluation of this aircraft revealed that the aircraft fell far short of expectations, both in terms of speed and range, leading to the major design revisions incorporated on the Tu-22M-2. This aircraft entered service in 1975 and has the NATO reporting name "Backfire-B". Almost 500 were produced in M-2 and M-3 configuration for Long Range Aviation and Naval Aviation units and are expected to remain in service well into the next decade. The light-blue two-tone color scheme has been retained since the disbandment of the Soviet Union.

SPECIFICATIONS

COUNTRY OF ORIGIN: Soviet Union
TYPE: medium strategic bomber and maritime reconnaissance/patrol aircraft
POWERPLANT: 2 x (estimated) 44,092 pounds (20,000 kg) Kuznetsov NK-144 turbofans
PERFORMANCE: maximum speed 1321 mph (2125 km/h); service ceiling 59,055 feet (18,000 m); combat radius with internal fuel 2485 miles (4000 km)
WEIGHTS: maximum take-off 286,596 pounds (130,000 kg)
WINGSPAN: 112 feet 6 inches (34.3 m) spread and 76 feet 9 inches (23.4 m) swept; unswept wing area 1892 feet^2 (183.58 m^2)
LENGTH: 129 feet 11 inches (36.9 m)
HEIGHT: 35 feet 5 inches (10.8 m)
ARMAMENT: 2 x 23 mm GSh-23 two-barrel cannon in radar-controlled tail barbette; internal weapons bay with provision for 26,455 pounds (12,000 kg) of stores, including nuclear weapons and free-fall bombs, or 2 x AS-4 "Kitchen" missiles carried under the wings, or 1 x AS-4 carried semi-recessed under the fuselage, or up to 3 x AS-16 missiles

Tupolev Tu-22M-3 "Backfire C"

The latest version of the Tu-22 in service with Long Range Aviation and Naval Aviation is the M-3. This aircraft differs externally by having wedge-type air inlets, and an upturned nosecone that carries a small pod on the tip. It also has a new radar (code named "Down Beat"), a new tail turret, and a rotary launcher in the bomb bay. The aircraft entered service with the Soviet air forces in 1985 and remains in service in large numbers with former Soviet states. Defensive armament is reduced to a single twin-barrel cannon, and most aircraft do not have the inflight refueling probe of the "Backfire-B". About 350 entered service, 240 of them with the Dal'naya Aviatsiya (long-range aviation), and the remainder with naval aviation units. The aircraft in Soviet service were noticeably short of any markings.

SPECIFICATIONS

COUNTRY OF ORIGIN: Soviet Union
TYPE: medium strategic bomber and maritime reconnaissance/patrol aircraft
POWERPLANT: 2 x (estimated) 20,000 kg (44,092 pounds) Kuznetsov NK-144 turbofans
PERFORMANCE: maximum speed 2125 km/h (1321mph); service ceiling 18,000m (59,055 feet); combat radius with internal fuel 4000km (2485 miles)
WEIGHTS: maximum take-off 130,000 kg (286,596 pounds)
WINGSPAN: 34.3m (112 feet 7 inches) spread and 23.4m (76 feet 9 inches) swept; unswept wing area 183.58m^2 (1892 feet^2)
LENGTH: 36.9m (129 feet 11 inches)
HEIGHT: 10.8m (35 feet 5 inches)
ARMAMENT: 1 x 23 mm (0.9 inches) GSh-23 two-barrel cannon in radar-controlled tail barbette; internal weapons bay with provision for 12,000 kg (26,455 pounds) of stores, including nuclear weapons and free-fall bombs, or two AS-4 "Kitchen" missiles carried under the wings, or one AS-4 carried semi-recessed under the fuselage, or up to three AS-16 missiles

Tupolev Tu-160 "Blackjack-A"

Another formidable aircraft to have emerged from the Tupolev Design Bureau is the Tu-160 long-range strategic bomber. Comparable to, although much larger than the Rockwell B1-B Lancer, the aircraft has variable geometry outer wings and two pairs of afterburning turbofans in underwing nacelles. It is optimized for high-level penetration, but also has a low-level terrain-following capability and has a higher maximum speed and greater unrefueled range than the B-1. Production of the aircraft, which entered service in 1988, has been curtailed by arms limitation agreements. Those in service have suffered from serviceability problems and flight control system difficulties. With the change in strategic emphasis for the CIS, the Tu-160 is likely to have a relatively short service life, although a handful of aircraft remain operational in the Russian Air Force.

SPECIFICATIONS

COUNTRY OF ORIGIN: Soviet Union
TYPE: long-range stategic penetration bomber and missile platform
POWERPLANT: 4 x 55,115 pounds (25,000 kg) Kuznetsov NK-321 turbofans
PERFORMANCE: maximum speed at 36,090 feet (11,000 m) 1243 mph (2000 km/h); service ceiling 60,040 feet (18,300 m); combat range with internal fuel 8699 miles (14,000 km)
WEIGHTS: empty 260,140 pounds (260,140 pounds); maximum take-off 606,261 pounds (275,000 kg)
WINGSPAN: 55.70 m (182 feet 9 inches) spread and 116 feet 10 inches (35.6 m) swept
LENGTH: 177 feet 6 inches (54.1m)
HEIGHT: 43 feet (13.1 m)
WING AREA: 3875 feet² (360 m²)
ARMAMENT: provision for up to 36,376 pounds (16,500 kg) of stores in 2 x internal weapons bays and on hardpoints under wings; including nuclear and/or free-fall bombs, and/or missiles including up to 12 x RK-55 (AS-15 "Kent") cruise missiles or 24 x RKV-500B (AS-16 "Kickback") short-range attack missiles

JAPAN
- KAWASAKI C-1 · 19

UNITED KINGDOM
- HAWKER P.1127 · 1960

SOVIET UNI
- MIKOYAN-GUR
  MiG-27 · 197

UNITED STATES
- BOEING B-52D
  STRATOFORTRESS · 1952

UNITED STATES
- CESSNA A-37B
  DRAGONFLY · 1967

UNITED KINGDOM
- AVRO VULCAN B.MK 2 · 1956

SOVIET UNION
- IIYUSHIN II-28 BEAGLE · 1948

CHINA
- NANCHANG Q-5
  "FANTAN" · 1970

UNITED STATES
- DOUGLAS B-66
  DESTROYER · 1956

UNITED STATES
- GRUMMAN EA-6
  PROWLER · 197

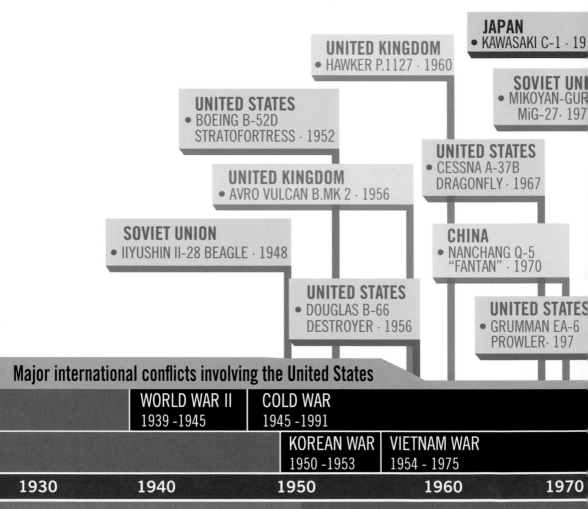

Major international conflicts involving the United States

WORLD WAR II	COLD WAR		
1939 -1945	1945 -1991		
	KOREAN WAR	VIETNAM WAR	
	1950 -1953	1954 - 1975	
1930	1940	1950	1960	1970

1960 - HAWKER P.1127

1975 - MIKOYAN-GUREVICH MiG-27

UNITED KINGDOM

SOVIET UNION

FEATURED WEAPONS TIMELINE

This timeline features notable advancements in military technologies by influential nations worldwide.

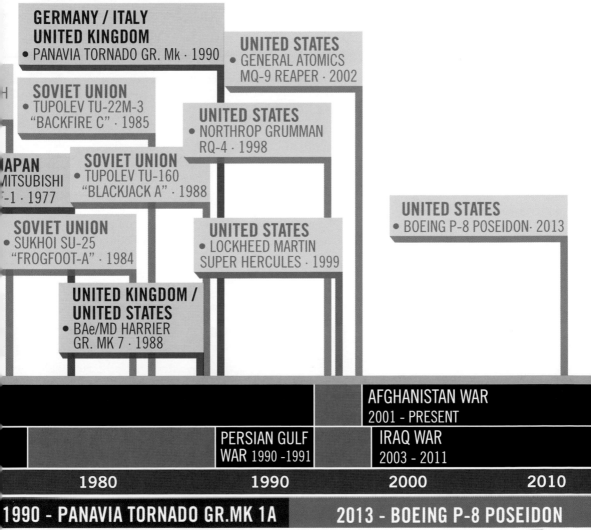

GERMANY / ITALY UNITED KINGDOM
- PANAVIA TORNADO GR. Mk · 1990

UNITED STATES
- GENERAL ATOMICS MQ-9 REAPER · 2002

SOVIET UNION
- TUPOLEV TU-22M-3 "BACKFIRE C" · 1985

UNITED STATES
- NORTHROP GRUMMAN RQ-4 · 1998

JAPAN MITSUBISHI -1 · 1977

SOVIET UNION
- TUPOLEV TU-160 "BLACKJACK A" · 1988

UNITED STATES
- BOEING P-8 POSEIDON · 2013

SOVIET UNION
- SUKHOI SU-25 "FROGFOOT-A" · 1984

UNITED STATES
- LOCKHEED MARTIN SUPER HERCULES · 1999

UNITED KINGDOM / UNITED STATES
- BAe/MD HARRIER GR. MK 7 · 1988

AFGHANISTAN WAR 2001 - PRESENT

PERSIAN GULF WAR 1990 -1991

IRAQ WAR 2003 - 2011

| 1980 | 1990 | 2000 | 2010 |

1990 - PANAVIA TORNADO GR.MK 1A

2013 - BOEING P-8 POSEIDON

GERMANY / ITALY / UNITED KINGDOM

UNITED STATES

Glossary

airframe
the body of an aircraft that does not
include the engines

arsenal
a place to produce or store military equipment
and arms

attack aircraft predation
unmanned attack plane that is controlled by
someone from a distant, safer environment

Cold War
a rivalry waged between the United States and the
Soviet Union after World War II regarding political,
economic, and propaganda issues with a limited
recourse to weapons

deploy
to place in battle

emplacements
a prepared position for putting a military weapon

fuselage
the part of an airplane that holds the crew,
passengers, and cargo

ground forces
military forces that fight on land rather than on sea
or in air

jet interceptors
a fast-climbing and maneuverable fighter plane that
can intercept enemy aircraft or a guided missile

light bomber
a small airplane designed to carry light bomb loads
over short distances

mach
a number that indicates the ratio of the speed of an
object to the speed of sound in the medium (such as
air) through which the object is moving

munitions
materials used in war, especially weapons and
ammunition

napalm
a gel used in fire bombs because of its ability to
stick to the target while burning

nuclear-tipped air attacks
a rocket or unmanned airplane carrying one or more
nuclear warheads

ordnance
military equipment, such as weapons, ammunition,
and combat vehicles

stealth
proceeding in a covert way

strike aircraft
a military attack bomber that can strike on land or
sea with more precision than bombers

subsonic
a speed less than that of sound in air at the same
height above sea level

supersonic
faster than the speed of sound

targeting systems
smart weapons, munitions, sensors, and processors
that can identify specific targets

theatres
the geographical area where war and fighting occur

underwing hard points
the area used for carrying weapons on aircraft

Further Information

Websites

http://www.combataircraft.com/en/Military-Aircraft/Fighter-Attack/

Information and images of military aircraft such as fighter, attack, transport planes, and more are showcased here.

http://www.howitflies.com/aircraft-of-the-day/douglas-a-1-skyraider

This site presents facts, specifications, and performance of the Douglas A-1 Skyraider.

www.mvpa.org/

The Military Vehicle Preservation Association is an international organization dedicated to the collection and restoration of historic military vehicles.

www.mvtf.org/

See one of the largest collections of historical military vehicles, overseen by the Military Vehicle Technology Foundation.

Books

Cooke, Tim. *Fighter Planes.* Smart Apple Media, 2013.
An up-close look at military attack and fighter planes used throughout history.

Donald, David. *American Combat Aircraft of World War II.* Motorbooks, 1997.
A comprehensive overview of the aircraft used by the US military during World War II.

Hukee, Byron. *USAF and VNAF A-1 Skyraider Units of the Vietnam War.* Osprey Publishing Company, 2013.
With its versatility, the Skyraider could deliver munitions to troops and inflict casualties on enemy forces.

Norton, Bill. *Boeing C-17 Globemaster III* (Warbird Tech Series). Specialty Press, 2001.
The C-17 transport can carry paratroopers and supplies in wartime or for disaster relief in times of peace.

Index of Attack & Transport Aircraft Profile Pages